# Contents

1

TESTIMONIAL

*"Thank you Donna Darden for these insights, gems and nuggets of brilliance. You have put your heart, money and soul into this important book. I was not only informed and inspired, but also empowered by your commitment, words and ideas on this critical subject of "mentoring" particularly in the Black community. I wish I had a M.O.M. like this when I was growing up. You have the answers and they are timely and needed. Bravo! We all now have something worth reading on this critical subject. Thank you so much for this powerful gift."*

*Dr. George C. Fraser*
*Author, Success Runs In Our Race, CLICK and Mission Unstoppable*

Preface

For over 20 years, I have graciously accepted the name of MOM, meaning mentor of many. Many of my mentees asked me repeatedly to write a book on mentoring. I admit, I have been reluctant to do so until now. Seeing so many young professionals needing help and guidance, I have become motivated to share real life experiences and questions from those young professionals that came before them. Life is not the way it seems and transitioning to several different positions is as common as an allergy or the common cold, much different than when I was in the workforce. The days of staying with the same company for more than ten years has come to a close. Anyone that wants to succeed in today's world will have to master the art of transition; embracing change and making it work to their advantage.

Throughout this little book of impactful wisdom, you will receive stories, followed with one-liners on how to cope with today's world. Basically, we know change is inevitable but very few of us have been trained to handle change so frequently. I am hoping this book will make you laugh, make you think, and help you to remember you are not in this alone; therefore, it is important not to take life and the small obstacles thrown your way too seriously.

Designed to be small enough to fit your pocket, purse, briefcase, or murse. (Man purse) You can refer to it whenever you need a lift, motivation, or even words of wisdom to ward off the evil spirits known as doubt. Doubt and naysayers lurk all around, as the true warrior, James Brown said. "Don't lighten up, tighten up! " James Brown, Godfather of Soul.

I am wishing you well on your professional journey.

As Karen stood at the foot of the bed, of the woman, her mother, who had raised her to adulthood, and watched her struggle with yet another convulsion, caused by the cancer that had riddled her body, Karen wondered what she would do without this very wise woman in her life. This woman that although she had never stepped out side of her role as a housewife, had equipped her children with boundless knowledge and skills to succeed in the worst of times. Karen was raised by a strong woman who taught her as a child to save for a rainy day, to pay herself first starting with her first profit from selling Girl Scout cookies, but this woman never had her name on a bank account. She taught Karen to read as she set the standard through leading by example. At any given time in the day, Karen would see her Mom reading. Karen's mother lived through books, and reading allowed what others would perceive as her mother's small world to transform into her having global understanding on many diverse subjects. Often, when passing mirrors at home, Karen would see herself, looking just like mom, glasses down on her nose, pen in hand, and book in the other.

Karen's father was just the opposite of her mother. He was controlling and possessive. As Karen recalled, her mother's only adult conversation allowed by her father, was with the next- door neighbor.

One day while visiting her mother's hospital room, Karen noticed her mother's eyes beginning to open, and she realized her mother was focusing on her. The TV was blaring loudly. Karen's father was watching his favorite show in her mother's hospital room. Karen witnessed for so many years, what she called her mother eating burnt toast. Her Mother had a habit of putting all others before her own needs.  Karen was a witness and understood how selfish her father 's actions were, and like her mother said nothing. The loudness of the T.V awakened her mother from the much-needed rest she was trying to get to escape the pain.

Finally, Karen, ignoring her childhood fear, asked her father to turn down the TV or at least turn it to a station her mother would enjoy. She could feel the tension from the large elephant in the room, her father. He was completely consumed in what pleased him and had absolutely no concern for her mother's needs. Once again, Karen was reminded of what she had experienced for years. When it came to mutual respect and love from her father to her mother; unfortunately, her mother's needs were considered with little regard.

Karen knew that her mother enjoyed a certain show that was airing then and suggested that the TV be turned to that station. In that moment, what Karen's mother said next changed Karen's way of looking at her life and changed her future.

Karen's mother turned her body side ways, as the pain she was experiencing was overwhelming and said with a very weak and soft voice, " Oh, it's really OK, I can watch it next Tuesday."

Karen's mother passed away the following Monday.

It was then that Karen stopped eating burnt toast, stopped putting off things she wanted to do for tomorrow, stopped accepting dreams as dreams and started striving to make them a reality, stopped allowing those that said they cared about her to treat her as an option instead of a priority and above all she stopped rewarding poor performance from anyone with reward.

This Book is dedicated to Lucille Leachman Darden, my mother and to all my mentors, M.O.M. 's that saw the passion in me to succeed even when it was not present on my shirtsleeve.

To my mentees , I say Thank You for trusting me to guide you briefly on your road to success. It was truly an honor and a privilege to do so.

> **Pay attention to your premonition---Use your intuition—and you will be positioned----For your transition**
>
> **Your Blessing waits for your admission**

## Impact One

# "No one can change your beginning

# Start today to make your ending!

**Going UP?**

Seems as if you landed the best job in the world, with great people, an office with a great view and a pleasant hour lunch, the people in the company simply adore you. Kind of reminds me of the elevator story, with an emphasis on seems like.

There was a young man who had been both good and bad equally while he lived his time on earth, and so was visited by an angel that was sent upon the young man's death bed to give him a choice of living his eternal life in heaven or in hell. The young man found himself being blessed with the power of choice, something like you have when deciding on your next job.

The angel offered; well let's call him Newby, the power of choice, to where he would be visiting first. Shocked, the Newby replied, "I never thought it would happen like this, I think I should get the worst over first; I'll go to hell." The angel nodded his head in acceptance and off they flew to what looked like a large elevator. The angel nodded once, and the doors opened. The Newby stepped in and down the elevator went. A few seconds passed by, and the elevator doors flew open. To the Newby's amazement, Hell was rockin'. Great music, great looking ladies, a wet T-shirt contest was underway and the Newby fit right in. He also saw many of his friends and was welcomed with open arms.

Soon, the week had come to a close and the angel stood patiently waiting at the elevator entrance for Newby. Newby appeared reluctant to leave hell and the angel, somewhat angry for Newby' tardiness, made one nod and the doors of the elevator flew open, closed and reopened in heaven.

Newby noticed everything was very orderly, the people looked rested and moved like old people, well older than he. It was peaceful, classical music played constantly, and not very much fun, but things got done and everyone seemed to be content. The entire week the Newby was thinking about his friends in Hell and how he felt so good with them. The work wasn't really hard, and there was no pressure to learn anything, like in Heaven.

At the conclusion of the week, as promised, the angel appeared, and posed his question to Newby. "You have had the opportunity to preview both heaven and hell, which do you choose?" Newby, without hesitating responded with a confident voice. "I never thought I would say this, but I want to go to Hell"

The angel bowed his head in acceptance and shook his head twice. The elevator doors flew open, and the ride to hell was quicker than before and Newby swelled with the excitement in seeing his newly made friends from the week past.

The doors opened with a bang and Newby went into shock. The angel standing behind him pushed him to get off the elevator. Newby, hesitating, said, "There must be some mistake, everyone here looks old, run down, depressed and the women, well gravity has taken its toll. I was just here a week ago."

The angel nodded his head and in agreement, whispered in Newby's ear in a very low voice, "Yes, a week ago you were a recruit, today you work here. "

**Impactful Moral:** Be careful what you ask for

**Impactful Mentoring:** Often our excitement for the spacious new office and the thought of the things it will afford us overrides our ability to ask the right questions before we sign on the dotted line. When you are new, you look like a crispy French fry, and alligators love French fries. <u>First question</u>: What is this entire package going to cost me?

**Mentor notes:**

1. Make good time of the before and after (What did the person do before you and what is expected of you now) Why did they leave, Why were they fired?
2. Deal with facts, statistics found in the company business plan, data on diversity numbers, etc.
3. Investigate, find a fit, talk with people that work there

4. Don't fall for the friendly face of the recruiter better known as the hype specialist
5. Take a look at the organization, if they are all young, chances are they leave before they get a chance to get promoted, I would ask the question Why?

## Ok, who am I to give you advice?

Why should you listen to me? I am sure you are probably questioning why you bought this book in the first place, and that is a great question and poses no problem to me to supply an answer. I was on a plane traveling to Cancun, as that is what I do as a retiree, travel, and I read one of the chapters I had just written, to a young lady sitting next to me. Ironically, she had just started her new job at the age of 18. Man to be 18 again and know what I know now. I believe they would label me hazardous material because I would, in a nutshell be dangerous and highly combustible as far as identifying all the unnecessary crap a new hire will experience. I would be able to maneuver around what I call the minefields of newness.

Anyway, there I go again rambling, which is just why it should not shock you that I am not a writer, yet, but more like you, a person who was the head of her household for over half of her life, raised two children, put herself through school and last job held was an Executive Vp of an automotive supplier, working my way up from an automakers assembly line. Oh, did I leave out the fact that I left school at the age of sixteen?

Yes, some would say, especially back in the 70's, I had all the odds against me. I learned to shut out the naysayer radio static and to listen to my inner voice that kept telling me everyone around me was in his or her underwear and his or her attire was not fashionable in the least. Actually, I told myself that we all get up in the morning and put on our underwear one leg at a time, unless you are really rich and maybe someone comes in and holds both your feet up for you as you slide on your 1,600 thread count fruit of the looms. In short, I have paid my dues and seen and experienced much.

I have a masters degree, and I have worked at two major corporations and I am proud to say that I have been MOM to over 23 mentees and over half now hold VP positions, own their own companies, or have been given partnerships in a firm.

I began to find their problems to be repetitive some years ago, which gave me the thought of developing this book and sharing their stories in hopes that their experiences might enlighten your professional journey.

Let's return to the young lady on the plane. She accepted my business card, tucking it neatly away in her wallet and told me she wanted to receive the first copy of my book. I think young people say it like this, she was really feelin'me. So as not to disappoint, this is my book. If you are reading this in Kindle than that means I actually sold two books. I thank you for your contribution.

**What is it Like Here?**

Sheila stood over her suitcase wondering what her attire would be to attend her initial luncheon with the President of Ford Motor Co. Her essay was one of four selected from over 1,500 essays generated from ten schools, and she had been granted a seat in the Ford internship program.

.

Sheila knew she did not look like the employees she would meet. Her father had fallen on hard times and her, and Dad were staying in motels and now she was living in her Dad's car, just barely managing getting to school and studying at the local library.

Sheila decided to wear her favorite baseball cap as she had no one and no money to get her hair styled. She added to her fashion statement, as it was warm outside, a tank top and some cut off at the knee white jeans. Her attire had just a little dirt on it, but there was no time to go to the laundry mat.

The other three candidates attending the kickoff luncheon were friends, so Sheila used her power of persuasion and asked them to follow her lead in their dress selection. There was one additional student accepted in the program, a young man, and he decided to take his money earned from cutting lawns and buy a suit.

As the young candidates entered on the 12th floor of the Ford world headquarters, you could see the employees of the company glaring at their misfit attire. Once they made it to the luncheon room, The President, although somewhat shocked, never let on that their attire was any less than appropriate.  He brought a new meaning to the story of the emperor and his new clothes. Some of the directors of the departments in which the four would be interning, turned to the intern's instructor and asked whether she planned to address their dress selection, laughing quietly. The instructor was not pleased with their ridicule of new candidates and quickly asked for a meeting after the luncheon to answer that question, addressing the concerned directors.

Soon, the luncheon came to a close and the instructor hurried to an adjacent meeting room to discuss what she had experienced with the mentoring directors. What she had to say put them in a different state of mind on how their ridiculing behavior affected the new candidates.

The instructor began to share the backgrounds of each student. One student lived in a car with her father; her mother had passed away a year ago. The second student lived in a depressed part of town, living with her mother, and eight brothers and sisters, the third student's background was similar and the young man was being raised by a single parent with his siblings as well. Sharing each student's story opened the eyes of the mentoring directors on what determination applied, resembled. The young man was accepted, although he did not carry a 3.0 GPA because of his persistence to making sure he checked with the principal's office every day for three months straight. The instructor continued and went on to explain to those that were going to be mentoring that the candidate's futures, they were being held responsible to develop, required understanding. The instructor made an example of the mentoring director's behavior that was openly displayed at the luncheon and asked, if that was the example they wanted to set. The instructor also went on to explain that these young people are in high school and in three short months it would be their job to prepare them for employment.

Upon leaving the meeting, the intern's instructor found that she had a committed group of M.O.M followers equipped with clear vision and objectives.

In three short months, the instructor watched caterpillars blossom into butterflies. So professional the candidates had become, by the day of the graduation luncheon, they blended in so well with the employees, that the President failed to recognize they were in the room. It was then the directors, and the entire organization beamed with pride.

**Impactful Moral:** Count your blessings. Not all of us have been blessed with the best or even the average, for those without; we have been given and achieved much to fill the void.

**Impactful Mentoring:** A key component of being a leader is to be curious about people. Ask questions to understand, seek to understand, and then you will be understood and your actions will be suitable. "Reach for their heart first and then their hand," John Maxwell

## What comes out of the mouths of our youth?

I had the pleasure of participating in a program entitled, Principal for a day. As the Principal you were given opportunity to speak with all the students within a 6 hours period on what your company produced. You were allowed to share what role you played in the company and mentor students on proper professional etiquette. I can recall a very angry bunch of young men. As I entered the classroom, words, descriptions on a racial level were being thrown around like a basketball in a March Madness warm up. Paper and pencils were being thrown about landing on whoever was in the way. I was met by a warning from the teacher at the door, telling me that this group had a history of being hard to handle. Stemming from his concern, he offered to stay in the room with me.

I found that to be interesting that a handful of young men, with water still behind their ears could generate such fear, or in retrospect, I thought, do I look that soft? I smiled at the thought.

Once I entered the room, I stood and noticed I received absolutely no acknowledgement. I stood stoic in the middle of the room as one by one, pencils began to stay stationary and descriptive words went to a whisper. I turned to the door and walked out, slamming the door loudly.

I entered the classroom as before, but to my surprise, as I made my action clear without saying a word, the class of so called unruly young men, were now sitting at attention and very quiet. So quiet that the teacher whispered to me that this was the first time anything like this ever happened. I went about reaching my objective, sharing my ten rules to succeed. The last rule was about proper corporate dress. Then, young men wearing earrings was not met with acceptance in the corporate arena. A young man raised his hand and said, " I want to make money, but do I have to wear those corny clothes and take my earrings out?

I began to share what I call my Piston story. I asked the young man, if you were on the Detroit Pistons, would you show up in a Spur uniform? Almost in unison the entire group

started booing and yelling, and laughing a resounding, NO! I then answered the young man's question. You can wear anything you want to wear when you decide to look for a job. You need to understand that the result of not being accepted for the position will be partly based on your clothing selection. There are clothes for pleasure and clothes for work. You can call it a uniform if it helps you to accept it better. If the corporate structure you are trying to get hired in, after observation, tells you that no one in the room has an earring, don't you think you should wait until you are a decision maker before changing the norm?

**Impactful Moral:** Advice is what we ask for when we already know the answer but wish we didn't (Erica Long 1942- present)

**Impactful Mentoring:** Always check out the landscape before you engage your lawnmower. You don't want to ruffle any flowers that have been there for years.

**The poor man is not always the poor man.**

I was working on my college degree and working at a truck stop as a waitress when God blessed me with this angel.

I had to walk a mile and ½ every morning to open up the L&K restaurant in Georgetown, Kentucky. I began at 6 am after dropping my 1-year-old son off at the sitters. It was a very cold morning as I remember, so cold the tops of my boots cut into the calf part of my legs. I made my way up the hill anyway to get things started.

Before opening the doors, I went about my daily checklist and watched as the morning crowd began to line up. Soon, breakfast had ended and set up for lunch was underway.

As usual, my favorite customer, Mr. Peters, slowly walked in taking his usual booth in my section, waiting to be pampered, as I had grown fond of him in the past 6 months. He wore a ruffled overcoat, his hands looked rough and his hair was always in disarray even where it had started to thin. He was short in stature, thin, and his shoes were worn and tattered. You could tell he lived alone and just needed to spend a little quality time with someone. I suppose I was that person, as I treated him like he was my Dad, always making sure he knew the specials and insuring he ordered a balanced lunch. No junk food for Mr. Peter's, the other waitresses would tease.

One morning when coming to work, I found myself locked out of the restaurant and it was terribly cold. The manager had failed to leave the key in the lock box. I immediately went to the hotel part of the truck stop and rang his room. I had no idea that the next few minutes would set me on another path unplanned.

The manager came to the lobby calling me everything, but a child of God for waking him and something in me clicked. I cannot tell you what voice I heard or from where, but it was clear that it was telling me to walk away. Walk away from the only income I had to feed my child and myself, just walk away. I started walking and reached home in record time because now I was fuming and second guessing my decision.

The next day about 11:00 a knock came to my door. To my surprise, it was Mr. Peters. I was so happy to see him and asked him if he had his lunch, of which he replied no, and I quickly whipped him up some mash potatoes, corn and chicken, his favorite. I was determined not to let him see how afraid I was so I kept up a good front. After he completed his meal and a little small talk. He asked what happened at the truck stop. I told him, he looked shocked and very displeased. He then asked what I planned to do. By now it was becoming increasingly hard to fight the tears, so I tried to change the subject. Mr. Peters reached in his old tattered jacket and pulled out a business card. It read: Jonathon Peters, CEO of Electric Parts, Georgetown, Kentucky. I was totally taken off guard. Mr. Peters was the owner of the biggest company, in town. I couldn't believe it. Mr. Peters asked me to come work for him and report the next day. I told him that I would be moving back to my home in Ohio at the conclusion of the school year, and he said, with a wide and comforting smile, you just report to operations in the morning and stay as long as you want.

**Impactful Moral**:  Treat all people with respect, they all bring blessings

**Impactful mentoring**: When one door closes another one opens... How you treat people in life depends on what that door leads to and how long it will stay open.

**Nobody Told Me**

I had the pleasure of a 911 call one morning by a young lady I will refer to as bewildered. She was going to be fired after 5 years of service and a recent transfer (upgrade) to another department. I asked her what prompted her to call me in the 13th hour, and her reply was I need help, something is not right.

I asked her when coming to my office to bring me her latest performance review. As I reviewed her documents, I could see it was riddled with poor attendance, missing meetings and not meeting objectives. It painted a picture of her head not being in the game. I found it very interesting when she told her side of the story, how very different it was than the perception that had been submitted to her upper management. Understand there is your story, their story, and the real story.

I asked her where she had been working before her transfer, where I might add that her previous performance noted her as an asset to the department and a model employee.  She, let's call her Candice began to go into detail. My first two questions were, what is it like, and what do they do?

I asked her to apply the same questions to where she is now. Her eyes began to glisten as she began to see the differences the exercise revealed. When I asked her about her tardiness, she told me she always started at 8:00. I quickly asked her to go back to the two questions I asked in the exercise, what is it like and what do they do here? Apparently, she had no idea of her new start time and apparently no one would tell her until her tardiness was in writing. Her answer to loosing her job was No one told me.

Now, I know reading this example is a little hard to believe, but it is true. How often have you failed to check the road before crossing? As a child you are taught to look both ways. This same exercise works in business. When you are given new assignments, a new position or leaving for a new job. It is important to ask the correct questions.

**Impactful Moral:** DO NOT ASSUME. It makes an ASS out of U and ME

**Impactful Mentorship:** Every job and every position comes with new rules, norms, expectations and start times even when they are in the same building or company. Ask the questions, what is it like, what do they do here. This is not college, there will be no bell changing classes, no calls from mom to wake you up, no bus to drop you off. This is your job and sometimes the foundation of your future career.

Here is a hint; if you get to work and the parking lot is full chances are you are late. If you get to work and the lights are not turned on, chances are you are too early. Understand the norm, how the team gets things done. Mistakes like tardiness get you labeled early in the game.

**Example:**  Mickey mouse could never get a leading role on CSI as an agent and Windex will always be known as a glass cleaner.  Be careful how you brand yourself. Point made, let's move on.

**Impactful Words:** On life's timeline

My Grandma's recipe

Grandma's Recipe

20  Know something

30  Be something

40  Have something

50  Be able to give something back

60  Have a good time watching others struggle through this process, they are not going to listen to you anyway, you're a dinosaur !

## <u>VISION</u>

# "Never believe what you see, SEE what you Believe."

**Opportunity comes in Blue jeans**

A good friend of mine, while I was consulting on a project said, "You know I think I get it now, you like hard projects." He had seen me attempting to guide a small company through a project and witnessed the resistance to change. The manager in the company was not supported by those in charge, so, I resigned my services from the project before what I predicted, the failure of the project materialized. My prediction

held true, and the project was not well accepted by the client. The small company lost the contract.

What I replied to him, I believe shocked him as he stopped talking for a couple of minutes on the phone. I simply replied, "It is not that I like hard projects, I am learning the true nature of why entrepreneurs and some business owners fail and I am gaining understanding on how to pass these pitfalls on to them in a way they can relate. I guess you would say, I want to experience a real life situation "

You see, I believe that opportunity comes in work clothes, like blue jeans. I attended a conference earlier where the speaker said he knew poor people. He said you know, People Overlooking Opportunity Regularly. Everyone laughed, but I found a whole lot of truth in what he said. Do you know any rich or comfortable people that pass up opportunity regularly? My point, exactly. I simply love to learn, no pain, no gain, no test, no testimony. Through adversity, we gain character, knowledge, and the ability to sense chaos and misrepresentation before it comes to our door. I can't point out the potholes if I have never traveled down the road. Who can?

**Impactful Moral:** Don't be afraid of holes, be concerned that you do not know where they are.

**Impactful Mentoring:** All that has ever been achieved has been highlighted through adversity. Achievement often requires a combination of courage and sacrifice. It is all part of development and growth. Don't take it too seriously.

**Adversity causes some people to break and others to break records.**
**Just go break something!**

# Impact Two

## "Other people, your relatives, and your friends, can

## Trip you up

## Only you can make yourself fall."

**Who's Yo Daddy**

Ms. Single constantly referred to the same Director's name when doing just about everything, from taking a break to reporting out in meetings. It was always John said, John said, John said.

One day in one of our mentoring sessions, by her request, and because she had started to feel pressure from some of her peers, I taped, with her permission, our conversation. I played it back and asked her to count how often she heard the word John. Within the first few minutes of the tape, she had counted herself saying the word John 15 times. As we counted together Ms. Single began to get the point.

A month later John was released from the company escorted out of the building. It was pretty ugly as many described it with major exaggeration. It was hush around the job on the details, but my mentee returned informing me, that she was experiencing increased pressure concerning her performance and her superiors and peers were setting her up to fail. Obviously, Ms. Single had been labeled as John's accomplice and his devoted follower; in short, the new click was out to get her. Ms. Single was overlooked when promotions came up and was put in loosing work situations with unrealistic objectives. Naturally, she was aligned for termination based on incompetence less that 30 days after John was walked out of the building. This pressure resulted in her employing an attorney and suing the company. She won the lawsuit because her facts were in order and through everyone's blind rage they had made some fatal mistakes. I saw it as a loss for the company as well as a loss for my mentee. She loved the company but was pushed into a corner with no way out.

**Impactful Moral:** Putting all your eggs in one basket leaves you hungry when the basket breaks.

**Impactful Mentoring:** 1) Don't reveal your mentors (Yo Daddy) Haters exist everywhere
2) Have no fewer than five mentors, one for every aspect of your life. 3) Go back to rule number one.

# Impact Three

# "Everything in life starts with one."

**Passion or Pay**

In finding flow, Michaly Csikzentmihalyi writes" Usually the more different a mental task, the harder it is to concentrate on it. But, when a person likes what he/she does and is motivated to do it, focusing the mind becomes effortless even when the objective difficulties are great."

We have all sat through motivational seminars where we have been urged to get up, get out and find our passion and yes we get energized only to be disappointed when we hit our job the next day. Not totally deflated, we write down what makes us feel good in one column as instructed and what kind of job we would really like to have, as our passion job, in the second column.

It is only after we see what passion cost that we start pumping the brakes and realize we can't live on passion, we need money! We are also introduced to the passion diet of four more years of college or possibly trade school to become good enough in our passion field to compete and then reluctantly, we write down what we have in our bank account. That part wasn't covered in the seminar except to pay for the four set DVD.

So how do people create or land the job of their passion? They are great believers in sacrifice at the beginning and they believe they will reap the benefits in the end. They are like eagles; laser focused with the ability to lock their wings and fly above the storm. They are deaf to words of defeat and possess a strong faith in their decisions and beliefs. Les Brown often speaks of his humble beginnings, sleeping on the floor of his office to makes ends meet. In the Pursuit of Happiness, the lead character tells the story of sleeping in the rest room with his son, as they had nowhere to go. Then there is the story of Joseph who was highly favored by the Lord, so highly favored that although his brothers were so jealous of him that they threw him in a whole to die, he was found and sold into slavery, and soon was favored by the pharaoh and made king.

Now here is the big question.

**ARE YOU UP FOR IT?  IS IT WORTH IT TO YOU?**

**ARE YOU JUST INTERESTED OR ARE YOU COMMITTED?**

**Impactful Moral**: If you want to play, you must pay

**Impactful Mentoring:** If you cannot be grateful for the bad times as much as you are for the good times, you might consider keeping your day job until your passion job comes along. Money does not make the world go round, but it makes the ride a little less bumpy. If you are sensitive to rejection of your ideas, your vision, and your beliefs, maybe this is not for you. Being and doing something you love is not for the faint of heart. It is long days and nights, and continual hard work. The advantage comes when you are working with your passion you have no idea of the time, and you are internally motivated to succeed and can identify your own achievements.

Commitment is the knowledge that the project you are willing to take on is doable and will get done. Passion is the stirring, burning sensation that moves within you to get it done, no matter what the cost. Commitment is about what you will do to the end, Passion is about what you believe and it has no end. Commitment is action; passion is a benefit.

# Impact Four

## (Old African Proverb)

## "You can't teach an Old Gorilla new paths in the jungle."

**What are you good for?**

Shelly approached requesting me to mentor her, as we shared a latte in the local coffee shop located in our work neighborhood. She spoke of others she had requested mentorship from and how they didn't call her when her Mom died and a few weeks later her Aunt died, and they said nothing. Shelly was very disturbed about the whole ordeal. She felt if they cared about her they would have called to check on her well-being. Imagine how she looked at me when I replied, I would have to think about her request of becoming her mentor.

The conversation began to get a little stale after my reply. Shelly abruptly said she would contact me in a few days to talk more.

Three weeks went by, and I received a text from Shelly asking my advice on an issue she was going through at work. I was very busy that day addressing projects, from what I called my real job. I then decided to write Shelly an email, as I could not reach her by phone.

I explained to her the following:

1) We both have jobs and as a potential mentee, as I respect your position, I am hoping you respect mine.
2) Texting is an inappropriate way to share information about concerns you have on the job, not only can someone else read them but they can also be misinterpreted.
3) A mentor/ mentee relationship is decided upon when both mentee and mentor see the value they both can gain from such a relationship.

4) Mentors unless they agreed, will not and should not be involved in your personal life. That is yours to share or in my case I like to keep it professional.

I concluded with the note asking Shelly whether it was really a mentor that she needed or a big sister or a friend.

A week went by, and I admit I was a little nervous in the fact that it was not my intention to be perceived as being negative with Shelly's request, but I wanted her to know how the process worked as well as possibly give her opportunity to forgive her previous mentor, after gaining a better understanding of what the term mentoring entailed. Her new understanding would support the fact that her previous mentor was not at fault. The following week, I received a phone call from Shelly. . It was interesting, as she stated that she did not want me as a friend, and that I was too old. She said her friends could be my daughters. I then very gently let Shelly know that I was not talking about myself, but addressing what I felt might be a better fit to address her needs.

She continues to have issues with the woman older than herself and continues to put things on a personal level. She has single handedly made enemies and caused her work life to be what I would describe as a train wreck.

**Impactful Moral:** Know that the very one you ask for help is observing you too. Mentors can promote and demote just by saying nothing.

**Impactful Mentoring:** Let's look at The Webster show. You know the very tiny black young man who constantly said, "What you talkin'bout Willis" Do you know that Webster was so well casted that he never ever out grew his role as Webster. He was Webster until the day he died. Sometimes we can step on so many toes that we are labeled, and it really doesn't matter what we do that is who they see and from that point on, to them that is who we are. People at work can be some of the most unforgiving bunch of people you will ever meet. Don't make your job an environment you plan to grow up in because it will stunt your growth. Sit down right now and describe whom it is you want to be seen as at work, and start today writing your script. Live it, Love it, Be it.

# Impact Five

**BREAK TIME**  Let's talk about your questions.

**How do I know I have the right mentor?**

You hate them and love them simultaneously. A mentor's job is to make you think, not make you comfortable or happy.

**What do I do with a mentor who was assigned to me but does nothing?**

Grin and bear it! Complete the process as best you can, do not praise, put do not put down the lack of effort you have experienced by your mentor. While your current mentor is wasting your time look for the other four mentors you are supposed to have, discussed earlier in the book. Above all do not burn bridges and don't reveal your mentor's faults. I know what I will say is going to tick you off, but allow them to take credit for the wonderful training they gave you even if you know better. The pay off often comes in finished things.

**Why should I waste my time?**

Just a short story: I had a student who was put with a terrible mentor. Every time we met she would tell me in her words the stupid things he would do or have her do. It wasn't until later when she was given a supervisory position that she realized that stupid mentor was secretly related to the owner of the company. She did as I asked and completed her mission. Now, the son of the company sees her as a supporter and she has complete job security. Nothing done is a waste of time.

**How do I find a mentor?**

Define what you want to be professionally and personally and then take who you are and find a match.

**What if they don't want to be a mentor?**

A great man, one of my mentors, George Fraser told me long ago, Kiss them, bless them and release them. He always told me where one is not for you five are for you. So get the one not for you out of the way, they are blocking the blessings.

**Is my mentor supposed to get me promoted?**

No, I wish it was that easy, but no, you get promoted if you listen and follow the instructions and guidance that are given to you by your mentor. It is all about you in this race.

**What can I share with my mentor?**

Agreed upon expectation between the both of you, job goals, career goals, vision ambitions, but please not all at the same time. All mentors are different, some will want to know what makes you tick and some will want to tell you how to tick. You take some of what you hear and make it work and if you don't like what you hear, replace it. Replace your instruction with what you think will work for you, staying focused with your eye on the price, the job you want. Invest in training programs to support your vision and by all means fill your Kindle with supportive research books that motivate you to achieve your goal.

**I've heard executives hire coaches, what is the difference between a mentor and a coach?**

A mentor will share work experiences and help you maneuver your career around the corporate mine fields. They are there to protect you and insure; the perception of you is positive in the eyes of those on their level and above. A good mentor should present opportunities for positive exposure and productive promotional projects to allow your skills to be observed and documented.

A coach does not share their experience. They listen and guide you to come up with options to meet the goals you are trying to achieve. They will ask for permission first to share their experience if you hit an obstacle and can't seem to move forward. Above all a good coach's job is to draw clarity of your goals from you and help you in staying focused to achieve.

# Impact Six

## "Don't tell a friend all you know

## Because one day that friend may be a foe."

Lucille Leachman (1927-1984)

**The Untouchable Boss**

Ron was a red headed, freckle faced new hire working in a sea of 25 to 30 year seniority employees. He was often set up to be the recipient of embarrassing comments at meetings and often the victim of pranks in the break room. Ron's story made this book because of his very innovative way of turning the tables to work in his favor, winning an untouchable boss's admiration, mentorship, and friend ship without utilizing HR to put a stop to his relentless peer group hit and run daily harassments.

First, let's describe Ron's boss. She was a woman who had to work hard for her position. She was constantly ridiculed and badgered on the slightest mistakes, which manifested itself in her leadership as pressure filled and pushy. Because of her gender, she did not welcome meshing with her peer group comprised of 95 % males. Her mantra was she was there to get the job done and did not find her work environment as a place that acknowledged her hard work or allowed and forgave the slightest incompetence.

Ron was blessed with great observation skills and a heart of gold. He was very active in his church, and it seemed his biblical leadership learning helped him to weather the storm of his peer pressure. He could be counted on to have a smile on his face and never, yes I said never saying a discouraging word to or about anyone. His boss had begun to notice how very genuine he was and how he handled himself.

It was about 3:30 every day, that Ron would see his boss in her office working on the next day's paperwork. He noted on Wednesdays she seemed to stay a little later, he was unaware of why, but took that into consideration. The following week, Ron decided to knock on her door and peek in to see how she was doing. He had his coffee cup in hand.

She was shocked to be checked on and hurried him from the office asking him to please leave the door open. The next Wednesday came, and Ron repeated what he had done in the prior week. Coffee cup in hand, he peeked in on his boss and asked if there was anything she needed or if he could help. This same process was duplicated for over a month, before Ron just stopped.

His boss noticed the first Wednesday he failed to check in on her. She shook it off as, oh well, but the next Wednesday, she realized she started eagerly expecting his company and his coffee cup pushing the door open at the end of the day.

The following Wednesday, Ron started again, only this time, his boss invited him in; she asked her administrative assistant to make a fresh pot of coffee just for him. From that point on, Ron was welcome to visit his untouchable boss and was the recipient of not one but two promotions in the coming years. She mentored him, and good mentors clear the way.

**Impactful Moral:** Persistence followed by constant Participation, results in Positive Positioning

**Impactful Mentoring:** A rough exterior usually shields a big heart of a protective and mighty giant. Observe and learn.

Impactful Seven

"There is a time in every man's education when he arrives at the conviction that envy is ignorance, that imitation is suicide, that he must take himself for better or

# worse, as his portion." Ralph Waldo Emerson

**Catfights leave undeniable scratches**

The door of my office opened and in walked a woman who had, still don't know the reason, hated me for years. She had been quoted as saying; She wouldn't mentor me if I were the last person on earth. She had returned from an overseas assignment, and now she stood in front of my desk, letting me know she would be the director of my department. Our differences came from, how I wore my hair or at least that is what I was told. She was a fair skinned black woman and wore her hair in a pixie cut. I was a brown skinned woman and wore braids. Yes, I said it; I wore braids. I had worn them since 1973. I was an athlete and braids allowed me not to waste time on my hair and dedicate more time to my health and my family.

It seemed every chance Carol got, in any open professional setting; she would make a remark about my braids or even more insulting come up and pull on my hair. Attention, all sistas know that you just don't touch the hair.

I realized I would have to be politically correct and somehow deal with this very different personality now positioned in my mist. I made a call to my mentor and accepted the advice she gave me. It was very short and to the point, just stay away from her, she will dig her own grave.

As months went by I found after careful observation and getting to know her through others that she had suffered a terrible trauma as a child and as I adored children, I was moved to accept her and overlook some of her vicious attacks. As my time in the corporation closed, I believe she learned to accept my braids and me as well.

On the day everyone was getting pink slips in my department and tension was extremely high, again, she entered my office and closed the door behind her. She wanted me to know not to pay any attention to the notice /opportunity to get an early pay out and leave the company. Carol told me that I was part of the team and that she had just visited the President of the company and something funny happened. I said, "Really? What?" She went on to tell me that the President asked only about one person in the department, and that person was me. She told me the President wanted to know about my decision and me. I laughed for a minute and said, " That lady is somethin'else, I'll give her a call". My director looked at me as if I said I was going to put a call into the President of the U.S and said, "No you can't just call her!" I stopped and realized that my director had no idea that the President had been my mentor for over six years. I had a meeting scheduled with my mentor the following morning; I shared that information with Carol. Carol asked that I give up my time with the President and allow my director to attend in my place. Naturally, when my mentor got the word that my department was being plagued with buy outs she wanted to have discussion with me one on one.

I allowed my director to take my 30-minute appointment time with my mentor, as it was the politically right thing to do. It is my belief that once the cat was out of the bag, they, those in the department were concerned that I may have shared some of the abuse I had received through my time with the company and even worst gave names of those responsible.

I was contacted by my President's (mentor's) administrative assistant. Donna, to come right up at the conclusion of her visit with my senior director. I had a wonderful visit, and we laughed for some time. I never shared with my mentor any abuse or any names. We always limited our conversation to where I was going, not where I was, and this conversation was no different. I was offered an executive on loan position with a tier one supplier who was not meeting our company's objectives. It was a minority company that I had helped internally to become the primary logistics company for all over seas operations. I was concerned about the reputation of the company and was torn in making the decision to stay or leave. My mentor looked me straight in the eye and said, take the position. Once our business talk was over we talked about family, friends etc. and I returned to my office and started packing. One week to the day, my mentor left the company. We still talk today. I miss her. She has gone onto bigger and better things and is happy and well.

The second week I moved to the logistic company.

**Impactful Moral:** You can't hit a moving target with a gun that has no sites.

**Impactful Mentoring:** The worst thing you can do is become a namedropper or a tattle tail about what is going on in your life and career. Depending on the power level of the person it can work against you. No one in the corporation knew that I had over three Presidents that I met with regularly and two VP's. I never took advantage of my position to throw dirt on anyone and paint a picture of dismay. It was quite the contrary, it was usually they that shared details with me and allowed me to brainstorm with them for solutions. I would say being in the mist of my power pack as I referred to them was the best days of my career. As mentors, they opened doors for me and those that witnessed my opportunities never knew where the suggestions originated. We had a secretive bond that has lasted far past my working days. The most important thing to remember is to protect your mentor as they protect you. Understand they are observing you and you should be observing them. Keep discussion topics on where you want to go and ask for the tools to get there. Your chosen power pack will play offense and defense, supplying opportunity even when you don't know it. A nod, a short statement, or even and email can move you in the direction of great success. Just don't break the bond and it will carry you through.

## Impact Eight

You may be enlisted in the war, but it ain't your battle.

When someone is looking for a crusader to go and tell the boss, because of their unfairness, the morale of the

department is at an
all time low.

Never miss the
opportunity.

"To SHUT ... To. .The ..
UP"   (Tyler Perry,
Maddea)

**Crusader!**

Greg was a great person. He got along with
everyone, and he could be counted on to listen to
the most disgruntled employee.  Greg liked how he
was perceived at work and relished in the fact that

he would make management pay if they were in the wrong.

One day he was visited by someone we will call Sally. Sally was new and seemed to be having some work life issues. She shared with Greg, that she had absolutely no time to devote to her kids with the mandatory overtime; their new boss Dave was demanding. You could often see Sally talking at the break area with others about her concerns. Greg took everything she shared to heart and decided he would speak with Dave about what seemed to be a very unfair move.   Prior to his meeting others were gossiping about how Greg would get management straight. Sally had alerted everyone in the office on how Greg had planned to meet with Dave later that day and she was certain that Greg would be very aggressive in his tone, when speaking on her behalf, and let Dave know his plan was unfair.

Like people do, many found a reason to work latter than usual awaiting the big boom that had been the main topic of discussion in hall way chatter all day.

Greg entered Dave's office and by now Dave had been armed with enough information to be quite ready for his attendance. Greg stated Sally's case as best he could, making suggestions to Dave on how he needed to handle the employees in his department. Dave sat and listened attentively. At the conclusion of the meeting, Dave stood and shook Greg's hand and said he would consider everything he said and that he would be putting something in place in the next couple of days.

It was Wednesday when Greg was called to HR and was given his pink slip. Dave had developed an overtime schedule to keep everyone working but because his employees were upset about the overtime, he was faced with the other option given to him by his superiors in lieu of getting the job done with minimal resistance. Dave decided to meet that task by reducing his department head count and dividing the work across two departments to meet an eight-hour schedule. So, this led to both Greg and Sally, low seniority employees, being cut from the team.

**Impactful Moral:** Crusaders often give their lives for someone else's cause. Ask Custard

**Impactful Mentoring:** Xenocrates (396-314 BC) says it well. " I have often regretted my speech, but never my silence." Their battle is not yours and unless you are an elected official ask them to take it to HR. Things get back to management faster than the speed of light and you will be handled even faster.

# Impact Nine

# "Not everyone understands the term, Lead by Example"

**Your Standards or There's**

The most powerful words said to me after 20 years of service, countless sleepless nights, missed time with the family, divorce and heartache, were, this is not your company. I sat down in shock, but the contents of the words hit home and released me from the developed loyalty I had to a structure that had no reciprocating loyalty to my dreams or me.

I am a visionary and often look years ahead when making management decisions. More than often I faced opposition. I was labeled as doom and gloom when the future did not look bright and like the Lord when he walked on this earth, I was loved when it was good and hated when the good ran out.

More and more of my mentees, under my tutoring, became victims of the same small minds, as they were being trained to read and predict visionary results, developing plan A, B, C for every possible outcome. It was called leadership. John Maxwell refers to this in his book entitled, The 21 Irrefutable Laws of Leadership. This is the first law called the Law of Lid.

Simply, if you opened a can and cut the Lid open halfway, how much can you fit in the can, but if you completely open the lid allowing the can to sit open with no obstruction, well, I think you get the point. It was then that I decided to seek a deeper understanding and learn about the human problem of accepting change, how to identify resistance to change and how to maneuver a win /win scenario when faced with that predictable opposition. It was during that time that I also realized that my standards fueled my passion to lead the company, and sometimes this clashed with the leaders of the company. Did they really want to change or was that a way to represent the company to potential customers, in actuality very little change would be tolerated or accepted. They were leading by their example and yours did not fit the program.

I started mentoring differently after this experience. After all, my mentees were being developed to be leaders and because of my mentoring, sometimes they were being perceived as predators, a threat to the current leadership's way of business. Most importantly, I knew I had to teach them the difference between their newly learned leadership and the current leadership level of the company. Something like if it looks like a duck, quacks like a duck, I would say it is a Duck. Unfortunately, companies that begin their new hire orientations, stating you were hired to change the status quo, translated, means; you can offer suggestions as long as it fits in our world and doesn't disrupt the norm. I have no time for you disrupting the current way we run this company and if you do, you will be harassed and isolated, and eventually you will quit.

It actually would be better if the opening orientations went like this, "Hey we need people, you passed the screening, Keep your nose clean, come to work on time, talk when talked to and don't disagree with anyone or anybody and kiss my ass now and then and we will have a long working relationship. Oh and don't ask any questions, because then you will be a problem.  If you take the time to join or be accepted by our current click group, this may work to your advantage, otherwise watch yourself.

Now, I know most HR people will have a real problem with that statement because they are the ones operating the elevator in the first chapter. Make no mistake; HR is there to protect the company, not you. Just remember those rose colored glasses they give you, like at the 3 D movies, must be turned in after viewing.

I decided to do a 360 on developing leaders in my corporate environment, and I taught my mentees to analyze the unwritten standards of their superiors, even if they found them not to be cohesive with their own, to honor those standards, and then position themselves for a higher level in the company. There and only there could they become the change they wished to create?

"You cannot fight by being on the outside complaining and whining. You have to get in the inside to be able to assess their strengths and weaknesses and then move in" Shirley Chisholm, First black female elected to U.S congress also Presidential nominee of the Democratic Party and famous for her tag, Unbought and Unbossed.

**Impactful Moral**:  Your job is different from your ownership, treat it that way

**Impactful Mentoring:**

1) Job expectation, to give 75%, not 110% the other 25% is to work on you
2) Decisions should be made according to the owners, even if they choose to ignore your information, so the buck stops with them. Your job is to notify them that the pit exists, but not to fight them or protect them from falling in it.  Look at it this way, some pits are made for people to crawl out of; this way they feel and see it for themselves. The lesson learned. Don't stand in the way of

their learning lesson especially if it will cost you your job.

3)    Loyalty starts and stops at home

# "Leaders see adversity as God's way of reminding them they are uniquely made."

**Mr. Big Shoes**

I am sure many of us after landing the new job or position have fallen victim to the, when Bill was here, Bill never did it like that, or Bill always let us use overtime if we didn't get things done, or Bill gave us time off when we needed it, or Bill, or Bill, or Bill.

A mentee called suffering from the Bill syndrome, and found herself intimidated by her older workers and the fact that she was a female, fresh out of college, working in a male dominate field, added pressure to her gaining respect and in turn meeting her performance objectives. Here is the story I shared with her.

One day early in my career being put in a position that seemed like walking in big shoes, I decided to act. I suppose it happened when one of my subordinates told me they called newly retired Bill, the person who held my position before me, and Bill told my employees they could work a Saturday of overtime. Several of my employees worked the Saturday and Monday morning I was summoned to meet with my superior wanting to know how I planned to pay for it. Naturally, I told him I did not approve any overtime. This was a union plant and once worked; the overtime had to be paid.

After careful contemplation, I requested a copy of Bill's objectives to show Bill's status of completion on all. Surprisingly, good old Bill had not met a single objective, but being part of the political network as I called it, he was protected and perceived as irreplaceable.

I removed all personal information from the Bill's review and called a meeting with his loyal followers. Most of them had over 25 years in the department and were not too happy seeing me at the helm. This included the supervisors who reported to me as well. After the meeting room was full, I began my questions, "Would everyone agree that you would go the extra mile for Bill?" All hands went up in the room. I then questioned the positive crowd, " Was it true that everyone loved and respected Bill?" A resounding yes, roared out of the, now standing room only crowd.  I then added the final question,  "So, if Bill was trying to meet any objective given, all of you would make it, right?" Yes, yes, yes mam, yes!

I asked for the entire group to look at what I revealed on the office board, which had every objective Bill was supposed to make and how he and the team did not reach a single one. I posed a fourth question, "Can someone tell me with all this love, support, and respect, how it is that Bill retired because he failed to meet every objective requested by his immediate boss and this company? " The room was quiet and filled with a large question mark. The Bill syndrome was no longer heard of again.

**Impactful Moral:** Imagination can paint a different picture than facts. Because the shoes seem big, does not support the fact that you cannot fill them.

**Impactful Mentoring:** If you do what you always did you will get what you always got, there is a reason you are in the job, make a difference, lead to change and above all, meet the objective repetitively. It is human to feel somewhat uneasy when walking on new ground. The only way to make it old ground is to make it your ground, one step at a time.

Know your worth, know your objectives and make sure your team knows their roles to support meeting those objectives. Do not assume because some employees have been there longer than you that they know how to run the business. A progressive profit seeking business changes constantly. Build a relationship with your people and your immediate supervisor, set up bimonthly meetings for updates on modifications to your objectives that your supervisor may feel you need to make to meet the objectives easier. Meet with your people daily to keep them updated and capture their concerns. Come with suggestions, solutions, and positive feedback. By the way, by showing interest, you will gain support, and respect.

# Impact Ten

# "The most important pursuit in life

# is the pursuit of the truth." Dr. Myles Munroe

**Talking heads over my head**

Ladonna sent me several e-mails she received from her immediate supervisor. As I read I could see a pattern of information being processed to leave her out of the loop. I called her to get the background information the e-mails failed to reveal. As I discussed the messages, I found that she had an older woman working for her and this person often updated her boss regularly. Naturally, when I shared the pattern with Ladonna, she became very concerned and asked for my advice on how to get this person to stop going over her head informing her superior. I asked Ladonna if she had experienced this situation before with this same subordinate. She told me yes and that she thought she had addressed it. The story I shared with her was as follows:

There is a stove in your kitchen and as a child you always want to reach up and see what Mom is doing. As a child you reach, and you get burned. I asked her to treat this employee like a hot stove. Ladonna's employee had been asked to stay away from the stove, and she chose to visit anyway. That visit needed to be explained to make sure the circumstances where not borderline insubordination first and if it was proven not to be insubordination, Ladonna needed to support her subordinate with an option to keep from getting burned by the stove. The employee needed to be updated about the burn she would experience and that you would do all you could to eliminate and keep her safe.

My mentee asked how she could do what I asked without causing a rift. I asked her to ask her subordinate the right questions? Number one; update her on what you knew to be fact and ask her to share her reasoning if it was true. Number two; ask her why she felt the need to repeat the communication to your boss, when she was asked specifically not to do so.

It was later revealed that the employee was being called by the manager and was put between a rock and hard place not to give information. My advice to Ladonna was to ask her employee when this happened again to update her immediately of what was going on, and to copy her on any e-mail sent to her boss. The outcome started a very positive relationship between Ladonna and her subordinate. For Ladonna, she learned to ask the right questions and not let anger guide her decisions. Her subordinate, gained a good boss that showed she would protect her instead of hurt her if there was an information leak. Subsequently, Ladonna set up a meeting to discuss her findings with her superior and her need to get information from her subordinate. Again asking the right questions with respect, her superior revealed to her a norm in the department where her subordinate was always the lead when certain information was requested. Ladonna then asked, since the information was now readily available, that she take that position for the department, insuring her value in the loop an allowing her subordinate to handle other pressing objectives in the department. Ladonna's superior was impressed with how she handled the situation and agreed to the change in the department norm, developing and publishing a department notification of the change.

**Impactful Moral:** It is better to think the best of people and allow them to prove you wrong

**Impactful Mentoring:** There are many layers to get to the truth, you can build or teardown in getting there, it is all up to you.

# Impact Eleven

"The Price of Victory is
High

But, nothing like the
rewards at the top!"

"Oh and by the way,
the elevator to the top
is broken,

So take the stairs one
step

at a time."

# Impact Twelve

"Experience and knowledge helps you to

identify and respect what you are

up against."

**Dragonflies and Helicopters**

I honestly can't tell you how often my clients have magnified their imaginations centering on what boss likes them and what boss doesn't.

How frequently they have looked for the unknown based on emotion, completely forgetting the facts.

My grandson was six when he ran into the living room and yelled, "Grammie there is a helicopter in the drive way. " I continued to read and work on my computer paying him very little attention. He came over to me and tugged on my sleeve, "Grammie there is a helicopter, and don't you want to see it?"

I removed my glasses, ran my fingers over my eyes and said. "Yes, Jay, Ok here I come. " I knew it wasn't a helicopter in the driveway but I love my grandson and figured I needed a break. Something flew past me, as we passed through the front door, coming down the sidewalk to the driveway. It was a loud buzzing sound, so loud that I ducked as we started on our way. Jay said. "Watch out Grammie, there it is!" I looked around to see a dragon fly with immensely large wings perched on a flower right outside the garage door. I looked at my grandson and quickly understood what he defined as a helicopter and why. Instead of telling him that it was just a dragonfly, I replied, "Wow, that dragonfly is as big as a helicopter, and then the question came. "Grammie what's a dragonfly? "

**Impactful Moral:** Don't go looking for helicopters when they are just dragonflies. Sometimes the smallest things look like the biggest things to certain people. Try to stay calm; it's all small stuff. Don't treat their concern as if it is a small thing even though you may see it that way. Solving the problem may be small for you, but your ability to solve it quickly will make you look ten feet tall in the eyes of the one who brought you the concern. Take advantage of the low hanging fruit.

**Impactful Mentoring:** As you manage people, it is your duty to acknowledge them with a good morning, not so much for them, but for you. A simple good morning, and transference of time, to gain information, could change the course of your day and your career. Never be too rushed to check in and hear what your people feel is important. Address the easy things first (dragonflies) and develop a routine of letting them know you heard them, you are addressing the matter and they will get an answer. If it is a pretty big order (Helicopter) ask them to remind you by asking you again in a couple of days. If it is something they can handle themselves, insure them of the proper way to do so,

who to talk to, what to do and how to bring closure
to the item and absolutely, ask them to get back
with you if they run into road blocks.

# Impact Thirteen

# "Success usually comes to those who are too busy to be looking for it"

## Henry David Thoreau (1817-1862)

**The Help**

One early Saturday morning after getting off work at 5am, I found myself driving from Ohio to Dearborn Michigan. I had heard about a new organization that was forming within the company, a resource group that would allow you free mentorship and offer classes to get you on track with company objectives. I was eager to get involved as I hired in, like in chapter one, the elevator stopped in hell and I was struggling to be accepted in a world that had no intention of doing so.

I packed up and headed on. I arrived a few hours later and entered a room of about 400 people. I couldn't believe that the company had so many people who looked like me. Each one stood and shared their department, their background, and their education. I can't describe how proud I felt knowing all these people worked in the corporation. As time went on, I began to build my network and utilized it to move to the Dearborn site. Once I was there I volunteered for everything that I could possibly do to push the awareness of the organization. It was my passion to develop people and the extra hours after work was not a concern for me. I was in short, too busy to be looking for success. Soon, I found myself in the movers and shakers offices; the presidents, and directors knew me by name. I was invited to close door meetings, and I was called on to develop programs for new interns. I was promoted twice and was what people would call on the fast track.

I had no outstanding skills, I wasn't what I would call outstanding, but what I was good at was leaving things better than the way I found them. I liked communicating, working with people and had no problem with running the show. I could make the decisions others didn't want to and I had absolutely no concern for those that, what I called blocked the blessing. I learned everything about networking through volunteering. I did not learn it getting my BA or my MBA. I did not learn it from my supervisor or any of the company offered classes' .I learned to observe, and how to execute programs through my mentors and the different assignments I took outside of my job. I learned from reading what successful people read and attended conferences that successful people attended.

**Impactful Moral:** God loves a cheerful giver and in the end your giving is rewarded with opportunity.

**Impactful Mentoring:** A resume takes on a new life when it includes donating your time. Volunteering is the easiest way to meet the decision makers in your company. Find out what charities your company supports and lend a hand, you will be glad you did. This is an avenue for them to see you in action and an opening for you to get up close and personal.

I've missed more than 9,000 shots in my career. I've lost almost 300 games. Twenty-six times, I've been trusted to take the game winning shot and missed. I've failed over and over and over again in my life. And that is why I succeed.

Michael Jordan

## Can you play the game or can you play the game?

I had a young man visit me at my office asking my advice on planning his career. I asked to see his resume. He had been with the company for more than 10 years. He was obviously good at what he did, and his performance reviews dictated in the same accord. His question was why couldn't I get promoted. I began to ask him a series of questions:

What organizations do you belong too?  Who have you volunteered with that the company sponsors?

What functions on site do you regularly attend? How many mentors do you have and at what level and position?  The young man looked at me as if I had insulted him and jumped up and said I didn't come here for you to tell me what to do with my time. I came here to know what I am supposed to do to get promoted.

I stood up as he was already standing over me and asked him to calm down and listen to what I had to say and if he was still not satisfied he was free to go.

I told him that Michael Jordan's high school coach told him that he didn't know how to play basketball, he was too short and he was cut from the team in his sophomore year. He looked to me trying to connect the dots. I said yes, he told him you can play basketball but you don't know how the game is really played.

I started to gain the attention of my visitor when I said you have the skill, but do you have the will?

My over heated visitor mumbled, the will? I said yes the will. You see. Michael Jordan took eight hours out of the day perfecting his skills and four hours perfecting his basketball relationships. His ability to understand the difference between will, and skill made him the number one athlete in the world.

**Impactful Moral:** You can have all the skill in the world, but if others do not witness your will and you yourself have no will. You will not succeed

**Impactful Mentoring:**  People who will themselves to jobs and positions do not sit in front of a crystal ball and chant until it happens. They resemble air. They are like everywhere. They work from sun up to sundown. When they attend a function, it is still work. I believe the younger generation call it Representin' They develop their networking skills to be able to turn any conversation to a subject they know and can shine in the eyes of others. They dress with confidence, walk with humility, and swagger (President Obama) and they invest in all they need to, they do the work, accept the work, and make it work. They investigate others, observe their likes and dislikes, and most importantly they present themselves to be curious about people. They listen, and people reciprocate by sharing something about themselves and along the way those same people supply valuable information that is needed to open one more door to success.

Build your will at the same pace you build your skill and you will be successful.

# Impact Fourteen

"The whole problem with the world is that fools and fanatics are always certain of themselves, and wiser people so full of doubts" Bertrand Russell (1872-1970)

**High Hopes**

Carl was a very intelligent young man. He stood 6'1 and held the stature of a college football player. He was personable, and everyone he came in contact with held him in high regard. Throughout his entire college career, his professors told him he would make it big one day. He told himself; I've done everything the right way. I worked hard to get my scholarship and put myself through school. I stayed out of trouble, done well in my studies, and now I have the opportunity for the best job in the world. I've investigated this company, and I know I will fit in. I will make this interview count. This was Carl's attitude going in. He was enthusiastic and full of life.

The first questions asked was what are your weaknesses and Carl replied, " I really don't have any, I work hard at whatever I do and I make it happen!" the second question was "Did you experience any problems getting here today? He responded, "Well, yes I did, the highway was cut off and I had to go all over town to find this place. It was hard to find." The third question was, why are you here, what do you want to do for our company in three to five years?  Where do you expect to be? Again, before Carl took a breath he replied, "I am here to become the best I can be, I am here to be doing your job in three years and I will be a director in five years. "

**Impactful Moral:** Really ????

**Impactful mentoring:** This is probably going to upset you, but, your goals are totally unrealistic and we all have weaknesses. In an interview it is best to tell a story, give your point of view. Like Six sigma. D for define the problem. M- Measure the problem, or the facts used, A- Analyze. Once you had the facts you started developing the solution, I – Implement, you put your idea in play and C- control, you reviewed your outcome, made necessary adjustments and it was positive. Stating you encountered a problem getting to the site and complaining about the road, gave the interviewer the idea, getting to work maybe a problem. Remember they came to work the same way. It appeared the everyday things bothered you. I think you know where I am going with this. This is the time when you ask me to role-play with you to reduce the shock of the questions and to get you thinking on your responses.

# Impact Fifteen

# "No weapon that is formed against thee shall prosper"; Isaiah 54:17

**The enemy is afoot**

It was my third week in what was known as the cushion room. It was the place all the seats for the plant were built and then shipped over to the main line for install. I can remember it was business as usual and as usual meant that every trick known to man would be played on me to sabotage the build of the units. The cushion room was notorious for eating up new supervisors and spitting them out. Working within the confines of the UAW was difficult, and fires had been set in the cushion room putting lives at stake.

I was put in the cushion room because I stepped on some toes, and it seemed the only way to get respect on the floor as a woman, was to think like a man, no relationship to Steve Harvey's book. I guess I need to be clear. In the 1970's a woman especially a black woman working in management was faced with a not wanted here sign, and my early career was no different. So those toes were positioned for me to step on them. If that didn't work my male counterparts would have developed something else to keep me fighting for every dime I earned.

Being put in the worst area in the plant, I decided I had to make it my home. I was a housekeeping fanatic, and the cushion room team was just the opposite, so I decided I could at least have a clean office. I went about getting the floor cleaned, and the windows of the cubicle scraped. The windows had to be scraped because the team would run the supervisor out of the office and eat their lunch there, smoking, and leaving food everywhere.

The first day the office was clean I went to lunch in the cafeteria only to return to a ran -sacked office with piles of garbage smeared on the floor. I was a little taken back, I knew who the culprits were but instead of showing anger I went about my day acting unaffected. The next week the office was cleared again and upon my leaving for my meeting, I locked the door. Prior to that, one of the culprits set his lunch box in my office. I notified him that I would be leaving for the meeting early and that he needed to put his lunch in the team center where it was supposed to be positioned anyway. He ignored me and when I left for the meeting his lunch was locked in my office cubicle. Upon my return, his lunch box was gone and the door was damaged. Again, I went through the day trying to think of a strategy that would slow this insubordination down. You see it wasn't that they hated me. It was my gender and color. The N word had appeared regularly on walls in the cushion room. I left that day at work ready to quit when something came to mind. I was excited about coming to work the next day because I had to see if my plan would work.

The first thing I did was locked my office door and head for the meeting. I remembered at the beginning of the shift that the culprit, Dave, brought and positioned his lunch box in my office. I warned him that his lunch box was supposed to be dropped in the team room. He acted as if I said nothing and left it tucked away in a corner, under my desk. When meeting time came, I had a security guard stationed on the next line. He watched my office and when the Dave pried the window, breaking the glass, he was taken to HR for destroying company property.

Ok one down. Then, I went around to all the black men in the cushion room and told them I had pizza for them at lunch time and that they better get to the office early before it was all gone. The plan worked, my office was full of black men sitting in the very chairs and eating on the very desk that the racially motivated group had occupied in my office. I watched as the good old boys entered my office with bewilderment in their eyes.

It cost me a week of pizza and Dave a week off work before I could do my job correctly. I remembered, my superintendent was afraid to come in the cushion room waving me over to the other side of the production line. He asked, "How did you do it? " I just replied, "The power of the Pizza!" and returned to my office and put my feet up.

**Impactful Moral:**  Never underestimate the power of food and fellowship.

**Impactful Mentoring:**  The quickest way to win the battle is to realize it is not a fight; the enemy has a chance of winning.  Choosing an offensive strategy will work every time.  You need to know the department process/, company procedures and the union contract. Using that knowledge to your advantage is the best way to be equitable. Notifying of the proposed change is important and giving opportunity for acknowledgement of that change is essential. It is seldom taken, but offer it anyway. Most importantly, Never let them see you sweat and know when you are nearly about to give up is when you will experience a major breakthrough.

# Impact Sixteen

# " You are an asshole when you prove to me you are an asshole."

**The Hunt is on**

It was in the middle of my workday when my office phone ran and a frantic, highly upset voice was on the other end. The voice was so frantic, and yelling so loud I hardly recognized it. After a few seconds, I knew it was Robert.  Robert was a newly acquired friend and working associate. He had over 20 years with the company, highly educated and very outspoken. He had run almost every department in the plant and was well known by many as being, the reverend. Actually, as I recall, our friendship blossomed over one of his outspoken moments. He was in attendance in a meeting I was chairing. I remember Robert standing up just as I was making my point on why people should join our resource group and Robert, subsequently, bellowing out these words. "Look I don't have time for a bunch of nonsense, if we are going do something than let's do it!"

Anyone else would have been a little intimidated, but I was very intrigued in finding out why Robert was so upset about the possibility of membership, and more important why he felt nothing was being done for potential members. Later, after the meeting, I asked for Robert to join me in my office and we chatted for almost two hours. He shared the unequal treatment that many of his team had been going through. He gave examples of people with skills being overlooked, and other managers coming in saying they were going to fix things, but nothing ever got fixed. At that point, I knew that I had an ally to help support my mentoring cause, better yet I knew I had an audience of people who needed to hear what I had to say, that being, how to maneuver your way through the corporate valley of the dolls. I liked the ring of it. It was Robert's idea.

Robert was yelling in the phone; he said he was done! They, the management at his plant had just promoted another good old boy over him to the superintendent's position, with a high school degree, As I said, Robert was a double master degreed employee and had been a first line supervisor for over 15 years. I tried to calm Robert down, asking him where he was and to take a few breathes.  Robert continued for at least 15 minutes sharing the terrible details of what he had been through, how HR was not supportive and how he planned to talk to an outside agency to level the playing field.  At that point I knew all I could do was just listen until he came down from the ceiling and I will tell you now, that ceiling was very high.

I asked Robert what he wanted to achieve by talking to the plant manager. He replied, " I want him to know what's going on."  I said. " What do you think he knows about you? "He said, "I am sure those low down... are telling him bad things about me and they are gathering the wagons as we speak. I heard they even called security." I took a deep breath and asked Robert. "What would make you think they called security?" Robert replied, " I left the building, I am in a phone booth near the plant on my lunch break. I don't trust them and some one told me they knew I was really upset."

I continued to talk to Robert to defuse his anger based on what someone told him and asked him to review the facts. I asked Robert, if it was a fact that the plant manager does not know him. He replied yes. Is it a fact that security was called? He replied, No. I then asked who is responsible for the plant manager not knowing you? Robert got quiet and replied, "Ok I see you are trying to make this my fault. His HR manager should be updating the plant manager about his employees that is not my job." I sifted through Robert's anger, and I continued to ask Robert questions, this one was, is it a fact that the HR manager did not tell the plant manager of your abilities. Robert said, "I don't know that to be a fact." I said, "But you do feel that the plant manager does not know who you are, correct? Robert, now at a depressed whisper said, "Yes Donna." I knew that yes, Donna all too well. It was a sign that I was getting him to think, and I could hear the wheels turning in his head.

I asked Robert to go through a role-play scenario with me on the meeting with the Plant manager, and not implement what he had planned. I asked him to think of himself as his own company, and the plant manager was a potential customer. We began to role-play on the phone. I raked Robert over the coals and played the devil's advocate on everything he was trying to share. I told Robert if he could anticipate the negative things that were going to happen to him he would have a better advantage to respond without anger.

I told Robert that chances are when he entered the plant manager's office; he would not be allowed to meet with him alone. The HR manager would probably be in the meeting as well as your boss's boss. , In his case, the Area Manager. I asked him not to allow this scenario to intimidate him but to enter the office with one goal in mind, to let the plant manager know what he brings to the table in education and contributing to the bottom line of the company. I asked Robert to be laser focused and ready for some stupid questions to be asked, just to pull him off his game.

Why stupid questions, he said. I told him, those that don't want to support you have painted a negative perception of you to all in the room that is why they are there. You, if you take this mission and your career seriously, must peel them back like a banana. You must put a question in your plant manager's mind causing him to question their report. Understand that when people hear things about you they automatically look for validation.

You will prove them wrong and a new perception will be Robert is a professional in every way.

Robert, now interested in meeting the objective I shared with him said. "Well how is that going to get me the job? They already filled it. I told him that he would not get that job, but he would be positioning himself to be considered eventually for something even greater. After some additional time on the phone, Robert agreed to give it a try. He realized he had to alter his mindset, discard the negative feelings and thoughts of them being against him and replace those thoughts with, everyone in this room wants to support me and I have something great to tell them.

A week later, I received a phone call from Robert. He told me that everything I said happened down to who was in the room. He thanked me for allowing him to role-play with me, because nothing they said shocked him. He was very pleased with the meeting and said the plant manager promised he would be getting back with him the next week. Robert said the plant manager shook his hand. This surprised Robert and replaced his negative feelings about his place of work with a new found pride.

Another week went by, and I noticed Robert had called my office several times. It was late when I finished my meeting so I contacted him at home. Robert, was overjoyed, he had been notified that he would be taking the superintendent's job the following Monday.

**Impactful Moral:** Two statements come to mind. "Quit cheating on your future with your past." Ann Golda Meir (1898-1970) said it best, "Don't be so humble, you are not that great."

**Impactful Mentoring:** Dealing with the facts, eliminating the emotional banter clears the path for a successful strategy. People's chatter is like radio noise, and it will give you a headache, resulting in your decision making power shutting down. Consider yourself as your very own company. Would you allow your company to be branded wrongly without a fight? How would you know the voice of your customer unless you met them face-to-face? People will tell you many things, and bad things travel fast. Dive into the facts and above all do not make others description of you a reality, unless you like it. If you don't have a mentor to pull you down from the ceiling, do the next best thing? Write down what you think. Read it until you have removed all the emotion out of your statement. Then look at the facts and see whether loopholes exist. In Robert's case, the question mark was in meeting his plant manager. He held the controls to give a positive image or what others in the room were hoping for and that being a disgruntled employee. He chose the road less travelled and ended up on the winner's highway.

By the way, Robert ended up being great friends with his plant manager. The plant manager was moved to corporate office where he received several promotions, and he continued to watch, support and mentor Robert's career until Robert retired.

# Impact Seventeen

"The secret of change is to focus all your energy, not on fighting the old, but on building the new."   Socrates

**Change, the six letter word that creates Terror**

I think we have all seen that dreadful list of things to happen to us during our lifetime and noted that we should all be called the walking dead. You know, the list of great fears that starts with, Death, Divorce, Loss of Job, and Public Speaking. What I find interesting is the number one killer, causing depression, and death is never listed. It is called Change. It ranks as the number one ingredient that can lead to both a negative or positive direction. Change can be terrifying, and at other times, you can find yourself praying for it. There are times when you know you should change and times when change will happen whether you want it to or not. Change is INEVITABLE.

I watched family after family break up after the massive layoffs in the auto industry. Wives no longer wanted to stay with unemployed husbands and husbands didn't want to stay with unemployed wives. I watched local food chains, and stores in our community closed their doors. I watch while people walked around the job riddled with fear, afraid they would be next. I had to release one of my employees and that same fear, which was highly contagious, was starting to take its toll on me.

Imagine working some where for 30 years and being giving less than 30 minutes to clear your things out of your desk. I found it even more disturbing when the lay off plague started to affect the executive group. Doom and gloom was having a field day, and no one was safe.

Soon, the worst was over and many of my working associates were on the outside looking in. I had been asked by a friend of mine to come talk with them about transitioning into new jobs. It was in panel form, and many that attended the panel discussion seem to get where they were, what they would have to do, and understood it would have to be done now. All were pretty much on board, except for one gentleman I knew very well. His name was David and he was in the last wave of higher management lay offs.

David was a very quiet, methodical person. He dressed the part of a corporate leader and had transferred from another automotive giant to land a director level position. He seemed to be very sure of himself. He came highly regarded and was part of the new management team. He defined himself as what was needed to turn the department around.

A word about definition: Don't be bamboozled into thinking you are defining yourself by the title you have accomplished. That title goes away and who are you then? Just another used to be, was or has been.

I saw David several months later, and he was passing out cards to his business where he was VP. I wondered as I looked at the card if David was experiencing what I refer to as, the once was syndrome. Being happy for him, I accepted the card and tucked it in my folder.

Several months went by, and I happened to be allowing the TV to watch me and a manhunt was going on in a part of town that I recognized. It was the high dollar district, no less than 1.5 million dollar homes. The news reporter was sharing a story about a young man that had barricaded himself in his own home and in his wild shooting through the door, had killed a police officer. I was in a hurry so; I turned the TV off and started on my way to meet friends at the mall. When I entered the mall, my cell phone rang, and it was one of my mentors. We chatted for a moment and then he asked me whether I heard about David. Suddenly, it all clicked. The David in the manhunt was the David I knew, and the David who had landed a VP job shortly after being laid off. Wow, I said to my mentor, Can you believe it? You could tell by my mentor's response he was shaking his head trying to understand what in the world happened.

As the story unfolded, David was supposed to be going to court for possible or alleged illegal funding in his company of over 350,000.00 and he had already lost his family and his house. It was a very sad story that ended in his 1.5 million dollar home being bulldozed and David being killed by police in his home. I found myself asking, what made him hold on to who he was? Why is it hard for people to see that they have the power to restart anytime they want? Why was it so important to be a Vice President? Do we define ourselves by our titles? What values and beliefs fueled David to hold onto something that was slowly slipping away? Did David know God? What was his personal Why?

**WHAT IS YOUR WHY!!!**

If you have been in any business classes, I am sure you are familiar with the "Who moved my cheese." It Is a great story of change. Two mice ran around with their shoes around their necks to be ready for anything and everything, while Hem and Haw, did just that, Hemmed and Hawed around not wanting to accept the fact that the cheese was gone.

What is your tool to accept rapid change? Take a moment and write down your WHY. When change occurs look at your WHY, speaks your WHY, and become your WHY. You will see that three letters extinguish everything you feared. WHY

**Impactful Moral:** If you can see it in your future, chances are you have a 50-50 chance of success. If you choose to go blind, your average plummets to zero.

**Impactful Mentoring:** Do yourself a tremendous favor and don't get wrapped up in titles and avoid drowning when it rains. The same people you see going up, you will see going down. I learned long ago, those that live in big houses have big problems and find it hard to stick all their stuff in a small house, so they work to keep things of little significance and end up loosing it anyway. When what you treasure is what you love and what you love, you treasure, change is like a flowing river; you just have to float to the next stop. Change creates opportunity and opens unknown doors to freedom. Be Free.

# Impact Eighteen

# "Returning to a position or job that did not appreciate you is as worthless as a blind man turning around to take a second look."

**Gotta Go !**

My phone rang one day with one of my students; Carol was on the other end. She told me that she didn't want me to be angry, but she was leaving the company. She valued my opinion and knew I had worked very hard to help get her positioned three levels above what she was in less than ten years. She was grateful, and I could tell in her voice, that her time at the company had come to an end.

It made me remember the first promotion she received, and she called, and asked me, "When do you know you should start looking for another job? I remember I said," Have you sat at your desk yet?" She said, " Not yet". I then told her, when you do, start planning for your next move. She laughed and knew I was serious. Anyone moving up the corporate ladder, like a trained marine, has to be ready for anything, willing to take on anything, learn everything, and apply all that to improvising when necessary.

Obviously, Carol had taken my advice seriously. She shared that she attended a meeting where the VP of Quality talked so rudely to her; she knew walking back to her office that she was done. I reminisced about how I walked away from a job and didn't even know where I would work the next day, and she said, "I know what you taught me and I have a landing place, never jump out of the frying pan into a raging oil fire, she mimicked me. I said, "So you are good? " and she said, " Yes, but as you told me, Take a vacation first so you can be clear and wash off the old job and the old norms so you can start anew. So that is what I plan on doing."

Carol did as expected and moved to another company rising from a plant manager to VP of Manufacturing in the following 3 years. The one key thing I remembered about Carol was her attitude toward change. She accepted that it was inevitable and that it was constant. Understanding that, she would go with the flow and her ability to look fear straight in the eye was the foundation of her upward mobility to take on unknown task. She was a change slayer.

Several months ago Carol told me, my old company's HR department had contacted. They were offering her a position to return. She called me and guess what I said.

**Impactful Moral:** You have to know when to hold em', when to fold em'. Folding is much better when you have another poker table in sight, and a seat is open for you.

**Impactful Mentoring:** Be warned by returning to a past bondage from which you were once delivered results in deeper bondage. Matt 12:43-15

# Impact Nineteen

# "Most trouble is caused by people that want to feel important." T.S Elliott

**Business or Bidness**

Adams Group was a small distribution company of about 250 employees. It was responsible for making and shipping body side automotive parts and distributing them to local buyers in the field. The company under went some growth in the past year and was up to be ISO certified in the coming months.

Tim was considered a handsome man and had been with the company for over 10 years. All previous plant managers' he worked under usually spent a great amount of time with him working on and reviewing his quality reports. Tim enjoyed the attention he received by sitting with upper management and wore it like a badge when he attended plant meetings. Because of that fact, Tim used his status to his advantage and had a reputation as being the ladies man with the female hourly workforce and was primed when he saw the new plant manager was a woman. He went straight to the office on her second day on the job and requested through her administrative assistant, to meet with her on urgent business.

The plant manager, we will call her Margaret, was from the corporate world, she was excellent in developing processes and believed in chain of command. She quickly told her administrative assistant to have Tim report to the quality director and that she would meet with all directors at the end of the week.

Tim was devastated especially since, according to Margaret's administrative assistant, she could smell him before she saw him, and his cologne was so strong. Margaret smiled has she received the information and never gave it another thought.

When meeting with the directors, she noted that the quality requirements had not been met since the last audit and began to question the Quality Directors commitment to the plant. A poor quality review would cripple the possibilities for future contracts. The quality director shared with the plant manager that his supervisor, Tim had always worked directly for the plant manager and that he, Tim was eager to meet with her. Naturally, Margaret asked the QC director what meeting with her had to do with his failure to meet his department objective. The QC director sat motionless as he gazed into the air searching for excuses. "Excuses are exits on the highway to success," Margaret recanted." I need you to get back on the highway."

Margaret reluctantly decided to meet with Tim. She found him to be overly involved in getting to know her and had arrived without a plan to correct the files that required updated records to pass the audit. At the conclusion of the meeting with Tim, she called the QC director. He had no understanding of the requirements, and the plant was without a doubt going to fail.

Margaret called a meeting with the HR director at which time she requested an investigation on the past audit and who was responsible to complete the quality objective. Her HR director met with her that afternoon stating that Tim was vocal in saying that she refused to meet with him, and therefore things were not getting completed.

Margaret sat back in her office chair faced with a problem. If she met with Tim, the entire structure of chain of command would be destroyed and the company would fall back into the chaos she had worked so hard to eliminate or, she would hold the QC and the HR manager accountable to get Tim on board to addressing what he was supposed to complete according to his position. Margaret had been warned that Tim was a friend of the CEO, and the CEO hired him.

Several months went by, and the QC manager reported data via a checklist stating that items were completed. Margaret, as well as the HR manager were beginning to feel comfortable about the quality status.

Because of the CEO had first hand knowledge directly from Tim, he requested an outside agency be contacted to review the QC records and assure a successful audit. What Margaret found out next was hard to swallow. Tim had lied about every milestone and when he was questioned why, he pointed to Margaret not wanting to meet with him. Margaret's feelings of fear, that sharing Tim had made advances at her, being perceived as retaliation, Margaret had to take everything her CEO threw at her to get things corrected. The audit results just squeaked by, barely making the objective. Tim would walk by her office making snide gestures, to insure that she knew what power he had.

What Tim did not realize was he had no power, There was a structure, and he had admitted he failed to perform his job and lied about the completion of work. In short, he falsified documents to mislead Margaret. He was let go on the spot.

Margaret could stop holding her breath, and the department started getting things completed in a timely manner and checkpoints were examined by the Directors to insure completion. Shortly, there after, the QC manager walked out as he had no clue on what his job requirements were and once his job description was reviewed, he quit.

**Impactful Moral:** If you don't confront poor execution or behavior, you endorse it. If you don't acknowledge good execution and good behavior, you extinguish it. Everyone on the team has responsibilities to perform, but the buck always stops with you.

**Impactful Mentoring:**  A review of job descriptions is always a good start with the implementation of reporting structures. Once those are made public, accountability and responsibility, to meet shared goals is clarified and identified to reduce friendship based business bias and deliberate sabotage to the company vision.

# Impact Twenty

"Remember, no one can make you feel inferior without your consent."

Eleanor Roosevelt

**So how am I doing?**

    Imani opened the door to her boss's office cautiously, as she was next to be given the annual performance review. She passed another co-worker as she entered and noted she looked sad and down. Imani really had no worries as she had met every objective and had received no negative information since her hiring date, 3 months ago.

Imani's boss was an older gray haired ,
stout looking gentleman that was known for
looking over his glasses instead of through
them. Employees teased that Mr. Shadows had
been with the company since the first brick was
laid. He was a no nonsense person who made
everyone around him feel uncomfortable.
Everyone knew he was a good friend with the
director so they kept their true feelings about
his inabilities to themselves.

Mr. Shadows made a gesture for Imani
to take a seat, and she followed his lead.  Mr.
Shadows began to review each objective giving
Imani very low marks and kept referring to the
gossip in the hallway chatter was that she was
too vocal about things in the company. Mr.
Shadows continued by stating that Imani was
discussing her salary with other new hires and
threatened to take her to human resources, as
discussing one's salary was against company
policy.  Imani was shocked and horrified of the
information she was receiving. Close to tears
she had no idea how to handle such negative
information and became defensive about what

was being shared. The more Mr. Shadows tried to convince her of her inabilities, the more Imani became intense on making him a liar. To describe the conclusion of the meeting would be like describing how the remains of a battlefield looked in Beirut. Imani was shocked, mad and horrified all at the same time. Her perception of how well she was doing was deflated in Mr. Shadow's description. She left thinking by Mr. Shadow's words that she did not belong in the company and was not worthy of a fair chance. She was completely depressed and hopeless.

Imani left the office that day bordering on tears and anger. As she packed her briefcase to bring filing home with her as she had done for the last three months, she wondered what the next day would bring. How could she work with such a group of backstabbing people? How was she supposed to face her director and the other supervisors now that she knew exactly how, based on Mr. Shadows information, they viewed what she thought was her accomplishments.

As Imani hit the unlock on her garage door opener, her little dog, Tyson ran out to meet her, shortly behind him, ran her 5 year old son and her husband stood in the doorway to the house. They were all smiles and ready to greet and have pizza as it was notably pizza night. Imani's husband could feel the tension emulating from Imani as she barely walked past him saying hello. He asked what happened to you? Imani, shrugged her shoulder giving off the signal that it was not something she really wanted to talk about. Chad, Imani's husband had seen that look before coming from her prior job and now it was back again. He insisted to know how she was feeling and what was going on. Imani burst into tears sharing every detail of how she was humiliated at work and how hard she had worked to meet everything given by her boss. She constantly referred to herself as stupid for thinking things would change.

Chad suggested that she phone her mentor and get some advice on how to deal with what Mr. Shadows was saying. Chad said he just doesn't know you so he is feeling you out. Imani, as she left the room to hit something, yelled out yes, all you men are always expecting us to react to your obvious bullshit and kiss your asses as we do it! Chad said, " well it looks like it is time for me to go to bed, good luck sweetheart, I know you will figure this thing out, " as he kissed her forehead and almost ran to their master bedroom.

Imani , after gaining her composure, began to dial the phone of her mentor, Anne. Anne had worked her way from the production line to executive VP of the company, and she had built a relationship with Imani for over five years. Imani was always careful when sharing difficulties with Anne, realizing Anne would also be forming a perception of her as she shared. Imani knew Anne to be fair and knew she would tell her if she was in the wrong.

After some time into the conversation Anne said something that turned Imani completely around. Anne said, "You are talking as if you believe everything he said."

**Impactful Moral:** There is only one way to avoid criticism; do nothing and be nothing. Aristotle

**Impactful Mentoring:** It is extremely human to be defensive when undergoing statements based on perception and not fact. It is extremely smart to identify the feedback given as just that, perception. It is responsible to view that feedback as 1) opportunity to capture and make changes 2) to own it and insure that the giver gets to know the real you, understanding that their perception is not based on what they know but who they know that has been talking about you. Most importantly, accepting with ease their mismatched appraisal and requesting information from them on how you can develop in the area they see your inefficiencies. Always set up a return meeting within the next week to discuss next steps to success. As much as I would like to tell you punching a dumb boss in the face would make you feel good. I am here to tell you that it is illegal and may have immediate gratification, but will lead to long-term consequences. Besides that fact, there are too many dumb bosses out there.

"I never killed anyone, but I have read some obituary notices with great satisfaction." Clarence Darrow 1857-1938

# Impact Twenty-One

# "The secret in greatness can be found in serving others."

**The Lapel Pin**

"I can't believe she wore that stupid huge lapel pin again today." Sharon shared with some of her co-workers as they stood in line at Starbucks. They all turned to look at Ladonna as she joined them in line. As they hid their snickering and gestures of displeasure, Ladonna unknowingly went on with her usual ritual, and ordered a tall mocha with soymilk.

When Ladonna's co-workers had returned to their desk, Ladonna was already hard at work and making her way through the office to pick up files. Everyone seemed to stare as she passed each desk; in awe on why she always had those huge ridiculous lapel pins on every morning. It seemed as if it started about a month ago, and even the supervisor wanted to say something to her about it, but felt it was a fad and something Ladonna would eventually grow out of and let go. As for the rest of the office team they were highly upset and became tired of being referred to as the lapel pin ladies every time the entire department met for general meetings.

Ladonna's fashion statement became so predictable that the office took bets on what color pin she would wear into work that day. It became a joke to most and a way to pass the time.

One day, Ladonna entered the office, and to everyone's surprise, she had no lapel pin. Everyone looked at one another with a puzzled look and quickly collected their money back from the office bets.

The next day came and still no lapel pin, everyone was trying to figure out just what was going on. Sharon, being the most vocal about the whole lapel pin thing was nominated by the group to ask Ladonna about her fashion statement and why she changed.

Sharon approached Ladonna, as she sat working feverishly on an assignment she had to get out. Hey Ladonna, what happened to your pin, we are all wondering? Ladonna turned to Sharon and with a very exhausted voice replied, " The lapel pins were from my mother; everyday she would pin it on me before going to work. I wore it because it made her happy." Ladonna returned to her work and Sharon pressed on asking, " Well, why aren't you wearing one today? Ladonna now staring out into space, replied, "My mom died two days ago and she won't be pinning anything on me anymore. "

**Impactful Moral:** Everyone communicates, Few connect, John Maxwell

**Impactful Mentoring:** Some of us have the highest IQ matched with the lowest EI (emotional Index) What does that mean? It means we always seek to destroy what we do not understand. We steer towards destroying something different versus embracing that difference. We do it to people, things, and through sayings, We hurt others because of our high IQ without knowing, we offend. A leader is curious about the people in their lives. They ask questions to learn, and they do not entertain perceptions, as they know perceptions kill.

A truly rich man or woman is one whose children and friends run to him/her when their hands are empty. Don't be full of you, be into them.

# Impact Twenty-Two

# "The future belongs to those that prepare for it today." Malcolm X

**Seize the moment**

I was visiting my brother not too long ago when the doorbell rang, and I witnessed something I think is a teachable moment. My brother is the head of a program portfolio of over 96 energy projects in the land of lights, Las Vegas. He and I were discussing strategies to address some of the poor work ethics he was experiencing with his newly hired group. As we spoke, he mentioned that he needed to find some energetic people to head up his outreach program, allowing casino owners the opportunity to receive an assessment of savings on their current energy bills through an on-site representative.

As my brother went to answer the door, there stood two young men from the local cable company. They entered the family room. One was named Greg and the other Darius. Darius was a true salesman and had an answer for every question my brother threw at him. It was obvious that Greg was being trained by Darius to get sales experience in the field. My brother was so impressed by this young man, without Darius knowing it; my brother began to interview him. He asked about his education, how long he had been on his job, and if he was interested in getting a better job. Darius answered everything quickly and was eager to find out more about the position. What I observed next is the bases of this last chapter.

My brother asked Darius, "What is your range? " suddenly that very confident and eager person went limp. He was unbelievably nervous and just blurted out a ridiculous amount. I recall my brother's forehead wrinkling and giving him a look like; you have got to be kidding. I wanted so badly to give Darius the range, but it was his interview.

After my brother closed the deal on buying the cable, he asked for Darius to contact him if he was interested in the position. Once Darius left, I recall my brother saying, if he had known his range he would have had the job on the spot.

**Impactful Moral:** Sometimes our greatest challenge is to be ready, when opportunity knocks.

**Impactful Mentoring:** We live in a microwave society where time is a luxury. If you have done the work and know what you want to do and what career you are looking for, you owe it to yourself to sit down and research the range that you expect to be paid. Don't be reactive, be proactive.

If you enjoyed my book, please feel free to leave comments on the Kindle website, ratings are appreciated. If you would like a one on one coaching moment, please visit my website www.perfectseminarsllc.com. There you can leave a message on my homepage and I will respond.


Take Care, Be Blessed and great Success!

CPSIA information can be obtained
at www.ICGtesting.com
Printed in the USA
LVOW03s2057080517

533738LV00024B/933/P